To: Audrey
Your the Apple
of HIS eye !
Sometimes you need
to be reminded
the fact their
loves you ! Ke
looking to t.
hills from r
where your r
comes from
Juanita
2/16/2017

Shh…Shh…
Mothers Are Hurting

By Juanita Day

PublishAmerica
Baltimore

First printing

ISBN: 1-60441-959-8 (softcover)
ISBN: 978-1-4489-7489-4 (hardcover)
PUBLISHED BY PUBLISHAMERICA, LLLP
www.publishamerica.com
Baltimore

Printed in the United States of America

To GOD be all the Glory!

To God be all the glory and honor!

I give honor to my pastor, Elder Phillip Watkins
Mountain View Church of God In Christ in Peoria, Arizona

I give honor to Apostle Joseph Brown
The Deliverance House of Miracles in NYC

I give honor to Pastor Leon & Co-Pastor Sandy Bohanan
New Hope Community Church in Covington, Georgia

A book dedicated to all hurting mothers in the world!
You are not alone…..Nobody talked about it aloud until now.

Cultured by: My mother Margo L. Day (Newport News, Virginia), Mrs. Clyde Correa (prayer warrior), spiritual mother Deborah Brown (NYC), First Lady—Lady Faye Watkins (Peoria, Arizona), DaVaria Roberson (best friend—Virginia), Missionary Takesha Turner (my editor/best friend/prayer partner—Arizona)

Special appreciation to Prophetess Winifred, Prophetess Nadine, Prophetess Emma & Prophetess Mel Amos

I thank all of you for being there as my support system for hours of listening, praying for me, over me, and with me. Most of all for not avoiding my phone calls. I love you and thank God for you all.

Sincere thanks to my uncle Burney who instills Godly wisdom to me. A constant strong tower that remains anchored in Our Lord.

Special thanks to my children (my babies) Shayla, Tommy Jr., and Ms, Kennithia—I LOVE YOU, always.

Special gratitude goes to these very special people in my life: Andrea Chaffin and Minister Alvin Q. Sheppard.

Great appreciation to my cousin John Marco Anthony Correa for touching and agreeing with me from the beginning.

Table of Contents

Prelude

The stipulations of being a mother…
***different depths of emotions**, the **different required levels of fervor**, and the **different amounts of concentrated fortitude**…*

Allow me to introduce myself. I am a single 42-year-old diverse African American mother. God has blessed me with two natal children; a daughter and a son. I am also the mother of an adopted daughter/niece (whose mother has gone to rest until the Lord's return). I always knew my children were my gifts from God above. I also knew God had given them to me for me to nurture, which would result in the ultimate return of the children back to him. There were things that I did not know about motherhood; which involved the **different depths of emotions**, the **different required levels of fervor** (obligation), and the **different amounts of concentrated fortitude** needed to accomplish and survive this honorable responsibility called being a mother.

From the beginning of time, being a mother was considered an honorable task. **The dictionary defines mother as a woman in authority that gives maternal tenderness or affection.** When we think about mothers we tend to think of a lady who gives birth to new life. Being a mother is a position we all admire because it has always been looked as honorable to and for the female. As little girls we grew up playing with our dolls, pleasurably mimicking the very behaviors we saw our mothers carry out before us. Years ago, in the 1900s, a demonstration of true **womanhood** was, if I may say so, to be just *half* the mother your mother was in her day, time or era.

Honor is given to traditionally celebrate Mother's Day by spending time with our mothers, which in turn makes them feel special. Once a year we celebrate Mother's Day by giving flowers, decorated desserts, gifts and even taking our mothers out for a special meal. Reminisce for a moment; are school children still fighting one another when a child speaks disrespectfully about their mother? How many of you remember the days when talking about another person's mother was fighting time?

Yes, I must say that being a mother is truly a high honor. Motherhood will always consist of birthing life, nurturing life and teaching on life while also watching our children go through life. (That alone is a set of encyclopedias with reference materials. Amen.) This new era cannot change!

Introduction

Reasons mothers are hurting...

"And I will put enmity between thee and the woman, and between thy seed and her seed; it shall bruise thy head, and thou shalt bruise his heel" (Genesis 3:15 [KJ]).

The year of 2005 has brought us the "finest of technology" and yet one of the oldest most honorable professions is hurting. Mothers are suffering without an ounce of world cure being sought after on behalf of the hurt that they endure. Yes, there are occasional talk shows that offer assistance such as boot camps for out-of-control children. These camps which are being sought after more now than ever before, are often understaffed or space is limited due to increasing numbers of affected children; costs are often unaffordable for the average family's income. Oh, did I forget to mention that these camps are for no less than six months per treatment term at the rate of an **estimated** $18,000 (ref). Yet, none of us have ever stopped to think about the fact that out-of-control children never were as big an issue before as it is at the present.

Perhaps there is an explanation for these out-of-control concerns regarding our children. Revelation 12:18 of the New Living Translation Bible reads, "Then he (the dragon) stood waiting on the shore of the sea." {At this point, John would see the beast arrive. The dragon (the subject of chapter 12) was waiting on the shore of the sea, ready to call out one who would help him pursue God's people.} (Ilumina-Life Application Commentary-Benny Hinn Ministries) As we read on, we discover that help does come from the sea to assist the dragon. An evil cohort rises in Revelation 13:1-2, "And I stood upon the sand of the sea, and saw a beast rise up out of the sea, having seven heads and ten horns, and upon his horns ten crowns, and upon his heads the name of blasphemy. And the beast which I saw was like unto a leopard, and his feet were as the feet of a bear, and his mouth as the mouth of a lion: and the dragon gave him his power, and his seat, and great authority"(KJ). Let's digest this information. The dragon (symbolic of the devil) called for help from one of his underlings, to assist in carrying out his vengeful animosity towards the mother. Now, this underlying beast to the dragon (resembles the Anti-Christ) has been given authorization to make war against the remainder of the inhabitants on earth. This gives clarity in terms of why mothers are singled out.

How can someone with such an *"honorable designation"* be experiencing mental, emotional or even physical heartfelt pain? The book of Revelations 12:13 reads, "And when the dragon saw that he was cast unto the earth, he persecuted the woman which brought forth the man child." The dragon which is Satan cannot return to Heaven and has in turn attacked women (mothers). Catch sight of the fact that women give birth and have presented a threat to the kingdom of darkness. Women, therefore, are targeted rivals for the dragon. If we read further, Revelation 12:15 lets us know Satan's exact feelings towards us. It reads, "And the serpent cast out of his mouth water as a flood after the woman, that he might cause her to be carried away of the flood." For the straightforwardness of Satan's intentions with regards to submerging us in sin refer to Psalm 124:2-5. He is an audacious challenger, full of overwhelming evil plans, which deceitfully consume us, and hinder us from having our names placed in the Lamb's Book of Life. "And it was given unto him (the beast) to make war with the saints, and to overcome them: and power was given him over all kindreds, and tongues, and nations" (Revelation 13:7). Honestly speaking, the beast is supposed to incite God's people, physically.

Well, why then are mothers hurting? "And the dragon was wroth with the woman, and went to make war with the remnant of her seed, which keep the commandments of God, and have the testimony of Jesus Christ" (Revelation 12:17). Mothers are hurting because of the curse placed on Satan in the Garden of Eden. There were two-fold curses handed out by God in the Garden of Eden; the serpent was cursed directly. The curse was to crawl on his belly for life. The second curse being, the offspring of the serpent and woman would be enemies, while the woman's offspring will crush the serpent's head, the serpent will strike the offspring's heel.

Chapter One

Hurting mothers from the past…

"Honor your father and mother. Then you will live a long, full life in the land the Lord your God will give you" (Exodus 20:12).

Let's take a look at the many women in the bible who we can consider as **hurting mothers**, the first that comes to mind was Mary the mother of Jesus. Mary was given a prophetic word by Simeon at the time of dedication of the baby Jesus. Simeon advised her that, "A sword shall pierce through thy own soul also." Mary was to experience darkness, as well as delight, as her "first born" went out to fulfill His mission in the world. She would see Him as the "sign spoken against." Manifold sword piercings were to be hers as the mother of the Lord (Herbert Lockyer. *All the Men of the Bible* [1958], *All the Women of the Bible* [1967], *Compilation* [2005]. p. 96).

These sword piercings (heartbroken experiences) came in the form of different confrontations and incidents and were all hurtful and difficult encounters for Mary, Jesus's mother. Often, she is referenced to as honored or blessed above all women found in Luke 1:42. Mary was well known for her characteristics of being humble (Luke 1:48), submissive to being selected by God (Luke 1:38) and was crowned with faithfulness (indicated by Elisabeth in Luke 1:45). She suffered agony while she watched her son (the blessed fruit of her womb) be persecuted for our sins at the end of his messianic ministry (John 19:25-27). It took much strength to stand under the cross and bear the corrupt mistreatment dished out to her son. This bitter cup, which her son endured, she jointly partook, being that she did not leave his side nor run to hide her identity as His mother. Mary was a true courageous soldier in the Army of the Lord and she received sanctioning remarks from her son Jesus Christ before he laid down His life. Mary exhibited a true example of valor for every mother to follow throughout life.

The second hurting mother that comes to mind is Elisabeth, the mother of John the Baptist. She was a devout advantaged woman of God. Having come from a priestly line and married to a priest, Elisabeth was a virtuous woman. She bore a son in her old age. We must keep in mind that Elisabeth was not only the mother of John the Baptist, but the first person to acknowledge Jesus Christ as her Lord in Luke 1:43. There can be no doubt that Elisabeth was grief-stricken after her son was beheaded by Herod Antipas, the Roman ruler of Palestine (Matthew 14:3-12). Imagine the heartache of seeing your only God given child murdered.

Hurting mother number three is none other than Hagar, the mother of Ishmael. She was unable to bear the excruciating pain as she watched her child lie near death in the wilderness from lack of water and food (located in Genesis 21:15). Hagar was forcibly removed from Abraham's household due to Ishmael mistreating Isaac in Genesis 21:9. It was here that Hagar symbolizes the Old Testament which is founded on the law.

Let's also take a look at Jochebed. The mother of Moses, Aaron and Miriam was hurt when the decree was ordered by Pharaoh to kill all male Hebrew babies, her son included (Exodus 1:22-2:10). Jochebed's heart had to skip beats as the soldiers searched her home looking for her newborn son, Moses. This act left Jochebed no other choice, except to hide Moses for three months until she could not safely hide him in the home. It must have been heartbreaking to place her son in an ark of bulrushes basted in slime and send him floating down in the Nile River (Exodus 2:2-3).

Hurting mothers of the past did not give up, but seemed to draw even closer to God, crying out to God more and louder. They seemed to have demonstrated unwavering faith relying on the fact that God had a plan and would work everything out according to His master plan and purpose. Mothers exhibited complete dependency on the Lord. They knew that God would show up and out on their behalf. Mothers were accustomed to leaning on the everlasting arms of the Lord for protection and refuge in all circumstances. What about us mothers, can we do that? **Yes! We can do all things through Christ Jesus who strengthens us. Amen.**

Chapter Two

It's a setup…know that God's plan will prevail.…

Could it be that the world has changed its values? Take a look at the time difference between Moses and Jesus Christ. The values have changed, but the antics of the devil were the same that antic being to kill all the Hebrew male babies. During both times, the order came from the rulers, King Herod and the Pharaoh to kill these male babies. **The purpose was an attempt to prevent chosen vessels of God from being born.** Did it work? No, the plans did not prevail, for it is in the book of Proverbs that God's plan for our lives shall prevail. "So shall they fear the name of the LORD from the west, and His Glory from the rising of the sun; When the enemy comes in like a flood. The Spirit of the LORD will lift up a standard against him" (Isaiah 59:19).

Maybe old principles aren't as important as they use to be? Let's just say that principles aren't the real issue here. Principles are just a focal point to occupy our attention while the truth is hidden under the surface. We need to begin to realize that time is running out. The enemy (Satan) is feeling pressured to intercept as many souls as possible so they do not get anywhere near Heaven. The enemy is causing pain and heartache in every way possible in the earth. We are clearly given this information in 1 Peter 5:8.

For certain this soul-winning warfare was serious in Peter's day and is even more concentrated today. Listen to this warning we were given, "Be sober (clear-headed), be vigilant (alert and watchful); because your adversary the devil, as a roaring lion, walketh about, seeking whom he may devour." **Listen** to the pattern that is used here. We are first tempted, which is why we have to be watchful and clear

13

headed avoiding temptation. As the devil walks about like a roaring lion, we are being sought to be consumed, engulfed, and or swallowed up. Sounds like we are in the middle of gorilla warfare for our own soul.

I ask, are we facing a cold hard reality that there could be a change in the generations, a *"changing of the guard"* so to speak, a guard which is attempting to revise our moral values in a down low sort of manner. What we are facing is just as Jesus explained in Matthew 12:25. "Every kingdom divided against itself is brought to desolation; and every city or house divided against itself shall not stand." The key solution to this problem can be found in Matthew 12:28, "But, if I cast out devils by the Spirit of GOD, then the kingdom of GOD is come unto you." Therefore if we allow our children and ourselves to be hindered from reaching the chosen level that God has set for us, then the plan of division set by the enemy has succeeded. Nevertheless, mothers, we must stand tall and strong because God promises to guide us and protect us. Furthermore, as Christian mothers we know that wrapping ourselves and our children in the Holy Word of God is our protection and the best weapon for security. For clarity, allow me to share an incident that took place not too long ago. I have a child who strongly walked with God during their early years. Yet, all of a sudden the very things read about in spiritual warfare books they began doing. Immediately, I felt in my spirit to wrap them in the word of God in prayer, since they were too involved in worldly activities to protect themselves. Praying applicable scriptures for deliverance from temptation was the best thing to do for my child's security in a time where strength in the midst of adversity was needed. Nonetheless, the bottom line is that **mothers** are hurting and what is going to be done about it?

Chapter Three

Invite Him in...

In these final days the heat in the fiery furnace has been turned up seven times higher. Let us not forget to be like the three Hebrews boys in the fiery furnace, have faith in Jesus Christ. Because once you belong to the Lord, He will show up and show out in victory!

One thing for sure is that the world may not be paying attention to you hurting mothers, but our Heavenly Father that sits high and looks low is attentive. Always remember that God is omnipresent. God is everywhere, all the time and he will work on your situation if you just invite Him into your life as your Lord and Savior. Just in case no one has informed you, being a mother induces a relationship with our Heavenly Father. Oh, by the way motherhood leads to a concentration in intercessory prayer for your children, too. Let us not forget that being a mother will have you on the altar repenting for your sins, ancestral sins and pleading the cleansing blood of Jesus Christ over the fruit of your womb. Motherhood will engender you, into the woman of God you were selected to be if you allow it too.

Let me break it down for those of you who are confused on this issue. God is the Alpha (beginning) and Omega (end). God created the Heavens and the earth. The earth is the Lord's and the fullness there of, the world and they that dwell there of. So in all actuality, we all belong to God. It does not matter whether we acknowledge God or not, we belong to God. Listen to this scripture for solid proof. "That ye may be the children of your father which is in heaven: for he maketh his sun to rise on the evil and on the good, and sendeth rain on the just and on the unjust"(Matthew 5:45). Whether we are His children (saints) or His creation the bottom line is we are God's, Amen!

We human beings were created in His image we have free will to join God or not. However, once we decide to join with our Heavenly Father we must learn and realize that our Father is a God of principles and not the author of confusion. His principles are well-designed and to be followed as instructions. A good example can be found in 1 Corinthians 14:40, "Let all things be done decently and in order." This verse reinforces the fact that God runs His kingdom according to principles so that all things are in order, leaving no door open for confusion. Now as citizens of Heaven (children of God), we must learn to apply the principles of our Father and His instructions to our daily life. Stated simply, we are expected to be obedient and therefore held accountable for our actions. Naturally, as His children we use His words in the bible and apply them to our lives for many different things blessings, growth, prosperity, abundant life, protection, wisdom, healthy family life, and our every need.

Now mothers there are principles regarding us and our children, instructing the protocol for all in the family. The Bible says in Exodus 20:12 **"Honor thy father and thy mother: that thy days may be long upon the land which the LORD thy God giveth thee."** Trust the fact that God did not say this to waste **His breath when speaking to Moses.** In Leviticus 19:3 it lets us know this is a **moral (ethical)** law it states, **"Ye shall fear every man his mother, and his father, and keep My Sabbaths: I am the LORD your God."** Believe it or not mothers are God's children, too. Children are gifts to parents and are not to be used for ill-treatment purposes. *"Behold children are a heritage from the LORD, The fruit of the womb is a reward"* (Psalm 127:3). Children (young or old) ask yourselves, "Are you acting like a **fruitful** or **fruitless** (harvest) reward to your mother?" Oouch!!

Hurting mothers are feeling upset, distressed, grieved, troubled, saddened, offended, and are aching on the inside. Mothers are being disrespected in actions, pushed to the side, verbally abused, and deeply stressed over this new generation of children who show lack of moral values, mainly respect! Yet we celebrate Mother's Day yearly; ironic, isn't it?

Mothers are being wounded and weeping all over the place! Mothers are being disrespected by children we gave birth to, incubated for nine months in our bellies and fracas in pain for them to have life. Mothers are crying themselves to sleep at night, due to pain from their own children that they carried nine months and birthed into this world. Mothers, Psalm 56:8-9 reveals scriptural promises regarding your tears. First, God collects your tears in a bottle; God is in tune with you even when you cry. Secondarily, God lets us know when we cry unto Him, and then shall our enemies turn back! Do you see how the scriptures relate to our daily lives? Comfort comes when we apply God's scriptures into our life experiences.

I remember once being told by a mother that motherhood did not have a good retirement plan. Are you kidding me? Mothers are being mistreated in ways that God did not intend. Today's children are so selfish, full of pride and rebellion, they do not care how their mothers are feeling.

For the Bible says in Micah 7:6-7, "For the son dishonoureth the father, the daughter riseth up against her mother, the daughter in law against her mother in law; a man's enemies are the men of his own house. Therefore I will look unto the LORD; I will wait for the God of my salvation: my God will hear me." Hold on, mother's, God will and does hear our cry. It may seem like there is no peace, but we do have a refuge! God himself is to be our place of safety in this present time of trouble. There are some things the world is not meant to handle, this is one of those things. We are being brought to a realization that God is our Alpha and our Omega! We are not our own! We were bought at a price and that's scripture! 1 Corinthians 6:19 says, **"What? know ye not that your body is the temple of the Holy Ghost which is in you, which ye have of God, and ye are not your own?" Jesus Christ our Lord and Savior was stuck, hung, bled and died on the cross for us, all sin, pain, wrong doings and all iniquity (wickedness or injustice) in this world!** (EDT).

Chapter Four

Motherly reflection... As the children transition (change over) in
life...my relationship with God transitions...into a dynamic prayer
life with God. A life that grew into a full life of my deepest request,
hopes, private desires and personal longings for my family, other
people, a nation of hurting mothers and myself.

Prayer *is simply having a conversation with God. We will have*
different types of conversations with God. These conversations can be
of an adoring (worship or praising) nature to God found in Matthew
6:9-10; intercession (ask on somebody's behalf) which is praying in
faith which is shown in James 5:15; supplication (requesting) as made
known in 1 Timothy 2:2; confession (admission of our sins) as expressed
in 1 John 1:9; and lastly a prayer of thanksgiving (gratitude) exhibited
in Philippians 4:6.

As I reflect back in my mind on this time period, I thought Oh my God,
help me! Somewhere my children where invaded and switched without my
knowledge. They were acting like strangers; complete opposites from those
that I'd given birth to! Don't get me wrong, when my children were babies,
toddlers, young children, even going through the start of puberty they still
seemed to be typical children, they were respectful, mannerable, and
reflected all that was nurtured and cultured in them by me. There was a
change that took place in my children which I never expected to encounter.
From that point on I began to search the Word of God for answers,
solutions to this change I was experiencing. Before long this would lead me
to an even closer relationship with the Lord. This growing relationship is
known as prayer, this had to be done before explanations would be made
available to me.

My carnal reaction was saying, "Was there a memo sent out that I did not know about on *changes in transitioning to young adulthood*?" It was like I must have missed something because I have been in their lives *everyday of every year* and did not miss a *birthday*! (In all realism, I needed to say what *spirit* is this that has manifested in my children **without consulting me** and is it ancestral? *Ha! Ha! like a spirit seeks your permission*.) Like the devil himself roaming to and fro seeking to devour their God-given destiny. Forgetting that Acts 2:17 reassures us that, **"And it shall come to pass in the last days, says God, That I will pour out My Spirit on all flesh; Your sons and your daughters shall prophesy, Your young men shall see visions, Your old men shall dream dreams."**

Know that God chooses the most unlikely candidates! *Beware, runaway children* like buck wild stallions, God has a way of **turning you around** to **his** chosen path. The wilder you are in the world, know that one day the wilder *you* will be **for and in God**! For sure you will be needed in this time which approaches this world, requiring extreme holy boldness topped off with a locked claw of dedication in Jesus Christ! For the Bible lets us know that **you children** shall be gifted in prophesy. You will do as God has destined for you to do. Read Jonah 1:1 through Jonah 1:17, where Jonah was being dealt with by God for disobedience better known as rebellion. Read about Saul on the road to Damascus in Acts 21:7-8, those who do not believe that God will show up and show out when you persecute **His** people (mothers).

For the record, I came from the **old school,** when mothers were respected to the utmost. In the epoch when a man saw a woman get on the bus or train, he relinquished his seat whether she had a child or not. If a mother had an armful of groceries and was pushing a stroller, without a doubt, any man would instantaneously assist her. My mother said, **"Do not do as I do child! Do as I say for you to do!"** I was trained that children were meant to be seen not heard. I was taught to respect my elders and **all** authority. Even my own mother respected her mother (my grandmother) in the same manner until the day my grandmother left this earth. My mother could have been 40 years old and if my grandmother said something that was it, with no thought of discussion or mouthing back! All it took was one glance from my grandmother and **we all knew** our place.

Bluntly put, my grandmother never physically abused us, as today's society would like to implicate. We were instilled with certain moral values and set expectations with no questions asked or deviations from those rules. In today's world it seems to be that children **(ages 11-32),** are just letting anything come out of their mouths to their mothers. Mothers are hurting due to verbal disrespect from their own womb; their children! It matters not if you are in the grocery store, restaurant table, rental car service counter, church house, driving along in the car, or even in the home you pay for children of today are talking to their mothers as if they are above you or equal to you. This new found level of disrespect is becoming more prevalent every day and it cuts deeper than a 12-inch dagger driven straight into your body cavity and protruding out of your back. It is a spiraling effect that can either lead to animosity (unfriendliness), hurt (wounded) or even anger (pissed off) with a touch of bitterness (resentment) equaling out to traumatic rage. Unfortunately, this effect is leaving mothers to seek for deliverance and healing from the Lord.

Reflecting back, old mothers did not need any male intervention, they used cast iron skillet frying pans to remedy **any** disrespect. Yet today, that is considered child abuse in the eyes of Child Protective Services while the real offenders go without penalty. Are we in the times of Matthew 10:21 when the word states, "And the brother shall deliver up the brother to death, and the father the child: and the children shall rise up against their parents, and cause them to be put to death."

We're not suffering so much of a physical death but an emotional death. Remember that we serve a God that sits high and looks low. A God who is omnipresent and his word lets us know that we shall reap what we sow. Be careful, our God is a just God.

It appears the children laugh, while the mother sometimes cries out loud as well as inside. Yes children will quickly say they are grown, yet they haven't seen anything in this world while speaking as if they are experts with PhD's. We have all heard them say, "You cannot talk to me like that; I am grown!" While they are barely able to vote and have not even signed their Selective Service cards. They may say, "You are trying to embarrass me in front of Betty or Jim." When the fact is that Betty and Jim did not carry you for nine months and give birth to you. Who cares what they think? Why do children feel that they can talk to us mothers out the side of their necks?

They have been given the power of, "If you hit me I am going to call the police and you will be accused of child abuse!" I witnessed an incident when a son about the age of 16 or 17, who somewhat over-sizing his mother began to challenge his mother's authority. The mother called the police and when the two police arrived one policeman took the side of the son and the other took the mother's side. What does that show our children who try to verbally rule their mother? The fact of the matter is the policeman's actions helped bring an upper hand for the son and a lower hand for the mother. Years ago the mother would have won the assistance of both the police officers hands down and the young man would have known to never disrespect your mother. I was shocked at the divided assistance between the male officers. Believe me that leads to deeper levels of verbal rudeness. We are warned a house divided cannot stand.

Even with all the hurt from your child's actions, **mothers will still miss them in those type of occurrences. Mothers still have the question of what are they doing? Mothers still pray for them with all their heart, soul and strength. Mothers still reminisce on the days when they were younger and things were different. Nonetheless, mothers realize that they have to be outside in the cold, rain, storms of their own lives which form and shape them into the very person God has for them to become. Many times we as mothers have to let go and let God, which is easier said than done. Mothers have pain as they watch their children go through their own necessary processing. Labor pains last for a moment, but hurt from your children is and can be ongoing nagging thorns. For sure there are days we would have preferred to stay asleep. This could explain why our own mothers objected to us having children before our time without marriage. Mothers have plenty of crying time. We seem to have buckets full of pain, hurt and sorrow. We have to continue to pray for our confused children, who are trying to find their way in a much different wilderness. This wilderness consists of AIDS, ecstasy, sherm, crack, crystal, rape of males and females, body piecing, sexual revolution at young ages, and search of independence and individuality at younger ages than before. Mothers who do not know prayer will get a degree in **prayer** due to motherhood, you can trust that! A relationship with God is a necessity, especially once you're a mother! If you think you can go this road without God, believe that you will draw neigh to the cross (coming into the light) and *moan, wail, cry out and seek* God for guidance, protection, peace, staying power and strength.

I am not sure which gender hurts you the worst, male or female children. I have one of each and I tell you the truth, the pain seems to be equal! Both can be disrespectful and rude in similar yet different ways. I believe it depends on which one is more stubborn in character and their methods used towards you. Males may give the impression to have more compassion towards females but can be very deceptive with their smiles. Females on the other hand have a tendency to be harder on another female with a straightforward method. I have seen and experienced many instances where daughters and mothers are at such unusual terms with each other. I remember a mother revealing that she felt like the daughter she had given birth to must have been transformed along the way into another creature (Chucky, the female version). From my experience, I can say that both hurt you just in different ways.

Chapter Five

My First Encounter—My Early 1980s Child

She was my firstborn straight out of college. I wanted her to be beautiful (inside and outside), to love me unconditionally, to have the advantage over this cruel world and to never hurt me.
What a tall order for my little princess to fill.
Oh, my vows were to protect her from all hurt, harm or danger and to cheer her along as she accomplished her goals in life. I swore to give her all the tools she needed to succeed in this crazy world. Looked forward to shared female bonding time of baking cookies and cakes. Sharing girl talk after her dates and dreading when her prince came to sweep her off and raise their family.

I must admit God granted me a beautiful daughter with long pretty hair. She was the joy of my life, happy, healthy and growing by leaps and bounds. Naturally she and her father had a close relationship. She had many of my qualities in her personality. She enjoyed dance, liked cooking, kept her room clean, did laundry promptly, loved to shop and it was a necessity to look just perfect going out. My daughter was an outgoing person with a normal social life. Once the children's father and I split up then came the change in my family. Her father was her partner to share with and she took the breakup and our relocation kind of hard. It was a big adjustment for all of us. However, she appeared to adjust to our new surrounding closer to my family. We had family support in case of emergency or crisis. I thought the transition was appropriate for positive outcomes in the children's lives.

Well, my daughter's grades began to slip drastically. She wanted to spend more time away from home with her best friend. I got a call from the school that I needed to come in and sign paperwork for her to get an evaluation. The school felt that her father's absence was affecting her education and life. When the report came back, I was too strong in my personality toward their father being out of the children's life. When he had a dependency problem and I refused to participate in that lifestyle. Well, my daughter decided to join a little gang at school and got jumped in at this crisis time in her life. I figured with all the family available maybe she would do good to have a family male as a mentor big brother. I enlisted my brother who was a karate instructor. This did help the transition for her. (Phew.—I thought it was the end of the world—thank God it worked.)

When she started dating a few of her male interests needed major improvements with their goals and focus for life. One boy was not cute and I could not believe it when she said, "Mom, isn't he cute?" The young man looked like he had just jumped up, put on his school uniform and did not bother to comb his hair. I said with a defiant shriek, "Oh no, where?" I do remember when I contacted her father regarding a male interest she had in high school. The young man was a definite no-no for my daughter. I was having trouble getting her to see clearly about this young man, so I asked her father to be of assistance. Well, her father agreed this male was not a candidate and we united against them being a dating couple. My concern was my daughter having any permanent bond with this young man. I felt he was going to attempt getting her pregnant. Being a single parent and working in a call center as management with flexible hours did not allow me to know exactly when I would be home. I felt if her father would have been in the home she would not have been tempted to have male company, when she knew I would be at work. Every mother knows that when she is away from home, the children will have company and try to get away with as much as possible. For certain I knew her younger brother would not tell me anything that went on unless there was trouble. I started praying for God to watch over my children while I worked to provide for them.

My daughter and I were at odds for years. It was a slow deteriorating situation with our relationship that took off like a rocket once there was a catalyst. This took place shortly after her first pregnancy which was at a young age. My one fear did come to life, although it was not with the same young man. (I thank God for it was not that first boy.) She was in high school in her senior year when I became a grandmother. Naturally, I wanted her to have a baby once she was married so that life would be easier for her. This young man did enlist in the military. I became a more cautious mother that felt like I failed in giving her the best life because I was always working. I prayed more than ever and stayed in church and was asking the Lord to step in and help me. I sowed seeds, paid tithes and paid my first fruits to cover my family.

It was the first November morning in 2002, when Jesus stopped by my house and escorted my granddaughter to Heaven. In my home that early morning, there were paramedic firemen on their knees praying as my baby lost her daughter. When I heard my child crying and scream out, "Why are you taking her away from me? She is all that I have." Looking at my daughter beat the floor with pain and confusion turned my hurt into anger but it was masked with strength. I looked to God for answers and I clung to the Lord like a child with their favorite toy. I felt like a powerless parent, who could not make this situation better or even disappear. The rocket of opposition departed after the loss of her first baby due to SIDS. It seemed like the more she grew into her stages of womanhood, the more we failed to agree on any topic. I thought at first it was going to be momentary, but it lasted for about four years. Sure I thought that she was rebellious, rude, selfish and out of control which made me think that this child is purposely exasperating me. When in all actuality, she was hurting and acting out by opposing me. She rebelled against what I cultured her to be, a woman who faced life with a reality factor. I tried everything to get my daughter to counseling so she would heal in a healthy way. **(This trick of the enemy was to upset me and keep me off course of my God given destiny**.)

Looking back I realize that she was pulling away to seek her own identity and to define her own distinctiveness. Nevertheless she **never** forgot the values that were instilled in her by me, which was a nice message I learned from this experience. See the Bible says, train up a child in the way that he/she should go and they shall not depart from it (Proverbs 22:6). Know that the word of God does not return back void (cancelled). We must remember that we serve a God that is the same yesterday, today and forever more (Hebrews 13:8). When it was God's time my daughter made amends for all the unrest in our relationship. **We** forgave each other and it took some of God's refiner fire for us to reach this point in our relationship. While going through this, I never thought I would see the day when we were merely cordial to one another. However, we have both developed stronger character, a stronger more secure bond with the Lord, a friendship, a respect for each others privacy, different opinions and unique individuality all done by the Lord himself in His time with His exactitude.

Believe it or not there are times currently, when we have conversations that grant liberation from our past offenses and close former damaged areas with invigorating restoration. God is **good**; I dare you to just try Him! Oh by the way, my princess did go to counseling and found it to be very helpful for her. Currently, she is happily married to her knight in shining armor with a happy healthy son and another child on the way. Oh, you know I still gave her knight in shining armor a rough time. He could not take her away easily from me. (Ha! Ha!) Nevertheless, she is successfully completing her degree in dance education. On her way to owning her first dance school with an auditorium, dressing rooms, dance classrooms with a parking lot for all participants. See we must learn to trust in the Lord; He knew the outcome all the time. I was the one out of the loop, reacting dramatically. Thank God for not being menopausal like us!

Sure I can sit here and advise this now but at the time of living this *I COULD NOT DO IT!* Frankly, at that time all I could do was be disturbed (crying, complaining and whining), asking her father what did I do wrong?

As far as he could see, I had done nothing wrong in raising her. His words today are that the kids had the stronger parent. (Whatever, man!) Why is this happening to us? I asked other mothers in the church advice. All man could say was go through it day by day, encounter by encounter or just leave her alone, it is a stage she is going through.

There was no correct answer found by people, but God knew all the time. What I really needed to do was pray to God for guidance. Read scripture for God's guidance through this—**"I will instruct you** and teach you in the way you should go; I will guide you with MY eye" (Psalm 32:5). I did not know that I should have opened my bible and read scripture for God's peace—"Trust in the Lord with all your heart and lean not on your own understanding; in all your ways acknowledge him, and he will make your paths straight" (Proverbs 3:5-6). Read scripture for God's strength—"Do not fear, for I am with you; do not be dismayed, for I am your God, I will strengthen you and help you; I will uphold you with my righteous right hand" (Isaiah 41:10). Pray and read scripture on that child of mine for God's protection—"When you pass through the waters, I will be with you; and through the rivers, they shall not overflow you. When they walk through the fire, you shall not be burned, nor will flames scorch you" (Isaiah 43:2).

Chapter Six

It started out like…
It is custom for every Jewish boy to be subject to his parents. *"He went down with them and came to Nazareth, and was subject unto them: 51a. And Jesus increased in wisdom and stature, and in favor with GOD and man" (Luke 2:51a-52).*
He was in right relationship with his Heavenly Father and with me.
Then came this sudden turnaround
My twister experience…

Mirroring back on my boy's life brings me to when he was first told by his father to watch out for me at the tender age of six years old. It seemed like a lot of accountability to place on such a child. This was the time when their father and I were separating. I never agreed with their father's actions regarding making such a statement. Excuse my train of thought, at that time I was very protective of my children, especially with their father! Mothers, you know how we are when the family is transitioning through separation. We have a tendency to shield our babies from all hurt and put up this strong force field against all potential danger.

At about the year of 1994 after the separation from my children's father, the children and I decided to leave Richmond, Virginia, and relocate to where my parents lived in Newport News. We had a family discussion and the children decided they wanted to be near their grandparents, aunts and uncles. I agreed with the children's decision; after all, I was an adult and could handle this departure from their father far better than my babies. My youngest sister was visiting us and she helped us load the moving truck and we drove the truck and my vehicle home. We moved from our own place in Richmond directly into our own place in Newport News; we had to maintain our independence for healing purposes after our family divided. My son was happy and loved being around all of my siblings.

I believe it was in 1999 that my children gave their lives to Jesus Christ. A decision they made on their own. It was at this time in my children's lives that I knew they were receiving gifts from God. I knew even though I was backslidden my son was called in Christ (Referring to Romans 1:6). There were times that I would hear my son and daughter say in unison, "Did you see that lady?" "She was a cat." Shortly after that I got converted in 1999, we began to have prayer and Bible study in our home. At this time, my daughter and I were reading the book of Proverbs to my son chapter by chapter with discussion for clarity. We knew that Proverbs is the one book in the Bible where God speaks to His sons and gives them wisdom. Once the children's oldest and closest aunt passed away we began to seek God for relocation instructions. Virginia had given us about as much negative memories as we could tolerate. We were seeking a new beginning to begin new in our lives.

We had moved from Virginia to Arizona by the time my son was 14 years old. He had grown up to love the Lord with his whole heart and soul. My son was excited about letting God use him for the Kingdom. He would help everybody and talk about the goodness of God. At this time in his life innocence was present and loyalty to God was everything to my son. You see he knew what God could do for your life. Take all the past negative situations and make them positive memories. I began to see my son sitting outside on the picnic bench, teaching the other young males about God and all that God had done for him. Sharing the wisdom he learned from reading Proverbs himself. Next, I would come from work and there would be knocks on the door by adults (on drugs or drunkards) asking for the young man who would tell them that if they believed God for deliverance from drugs or alcohol it would be done. Many people in our neighborhood sought for counsel on their addictions, prayer and even advice. Countless times my son would spend hours on end talking with people about the goodness of God.

As I recall there were three incidents, where I saw my son walk stronger with the Lord than most adults. The first one was when I witnessed my son in a year-long court case against a grown man who had racially harassed him every day to the point of tears, tell the judge that the God he serves says vengeance towards our enemies belongs to the Lord. The judge commended me on bringing my children up in the ways of the Lord and threw the book at the man. My second occasion was when I felt led to go down to my son's school to check up on him without him being warned. I parked in the drug store parking lot unnoticed and I saw my son feeding the homeless people on the street in that area, chicken from Churches. I sat in my car amazed and said thank you Lord with tears rolling down my face. When he came home from school, I gave him all the cash I had on me for school the next day. He had a worthy cause going on down there and I wanted to help feed the homeless too. I never mentioned to him what I saw until this book and he reads it for himself. Finally the last example completely astonished me. I was in pain in my body and could not move to drive nor could I get up from my bed. My son took the bottle of anointed oil in our home, got the Bible and began to read scripture. Led by the Holy Spirit my son laid hands on me and had my niece touch and agree with him for my healing. Believe it or not the next morning the pain was gone and I gave that testimony in church.

Somewhere around my son's 17th year, after attending seminary school and a community college there seemed to be a change in him towards life. He began to talk less about God, hang out more with friends and lean more towards worldly interests than ever before. On the day he turned 18 years old my son walked in the door with a tattoo of Psalm 23 and soon to follow was a totally different attitude. I was unnerved at the fact that this was a completely different turn in his character. My first thought was where is my son? He looked like him, spoke like him and walked like him but his actions where totally different. I said, My God where is my boy? The one who listened to your voice and followed every word you gave to him. My son the one who would be master of ceremony at our church on Youth Sunday and pray corporately until God would show up. I felt as if the bottom of my world had just dropped out and was leaking all over the place.

Naturally, as any mother would I began to pray and ask God to help me with this change with my son. It looked like the more I travailed out in prayer to God the further my son ran away from me and our home. Nothing I seemed to say to him agreed with him. He spent more nights away from home partying until he moved in with his sister. See I knew the ancestral bondage that followed in his father's line. I did not want those same hindering spirits to attack my son and devour him like they had done to the children's father. Oh,

I fasted, prayed, cried, got upset, got angry, and even denied some of the behaviors exhibited towards me by my son.

Often there would be disagreements followed by shouting matches, followed by walkouts on discussions and then no communication for time periods. The spirit of division was attacking my family and I did not do anything about it because I had hurt feelings and an attitude. Talk about having the wisdom, the ability and knowledge then not using it to win the battle; that was exactly what I did. I was so engulfed with emotions that my logic, street survival instincts did not come alive in me. Honestly, mothers, the enemy knows just how hard to hit you and exactly where to hit you. The blow given to us by the enemy is designed to throw you off course, but the key to victory is to rise back up after you have recuperated. While you're down get some warfare scriptures (Psalms 4, 5, 11, 28, 41, 55, 59, 64, 70, 109, 120, 140, 141 and 143) in your spirit, listen to the Spirit of God as you are being advised and develop a strategy for victory.

We allow the Devil to make a fool out of us every chance we get. It is time to change the roles here and fight back with scripture, binding and loosing strongholds, praying, fasting and consecration. That means do not be on the phone telling Betty, Sue and Pam. God is on call 24 hours a day all seven days a week. Go to church, get on that altar, have prayer for your family by the elders, sow some financial deliverance seeds in fertile ground for a successful harvest in due season and keep your eyes stayed on God. I dare you to just try God. God will not leave you or back out on His promises. He's never failed any one of us yet.

Now as for the situations which occur from our male children, as I stated earlier male children seem to serve their deceptive mannerisms with a mountain-size false smile. They definitely need that **vital male role model** or else you may get a more intense battle. Males have a tendency to be seeking to find their way between what the world holds as ideal for them and what mothers want and require of them. Difficulty in finding that unique comfortable medium is the problem. Keeping in mind that males like to aggravate, irritate and tease while they are doing whatever it is they choose to do at that particular time which is callousness to us as women. My own child really hates me, were my feelings and thoughts!

To watch my son change from this love of his mother to pluck my every nerve on purpose and oppose me on every hand was crushing to the mind and heart. (Remember that women are emotional creatures by nature.) Pray, mothers, knowing that justice comes from the Lord. Proverbs 29:17 says *"correct your son, and he will give you rest; Yes, he will give delight to your soul."* Sons tend to be openly defiant on every issue. To the point that I had to let him go out of my door with tears rolling down my face—praying that God would just take over at that moment. "Crying out GOD, you said that the thief does not come except to steal, and to kill, and destroy my boy. Yet, YOU LORD have come so that my boy may have life, and that he may have it more abundantly. For you are the GOOD Shepherd like in Psalm 22! The GOOD Shepherd who gave his life for the sheep" (John 10:10-11).

See I had to realize that I could raise him up on how he should be (we read the book of Proverbs every summer together for years so he could know God's wisdom for life), give him all the tools (education, hands-on financial management, structured reading *He-motions* by T.D. Jakes), physical defense classes (karate) to grow up with but, **I could not transition him to manhood.** A crushing reality was that I could never know how to do this with him, for I am woman. Remember that males are growing to be spiritual heads, which requires a head to do the job correctly. One thing with males is that if you let them bump their own heads long enough **again** and **again**, once they get tired and they lose enough they will stop on their own free will.

Just remember to keep praying against their negative mannerisms to be transformed into positive actions. Pray for God to protect them, guide them and for God to deliver them fully. Know that our eternal God is your refuge, and underneath are His everlasting arms; He will thrust out the enemy from before you, and will say, "Destroy!" according to Deuteronomy 33:27. Believe it, speak it and receive it for God is not a man that he should lie. Today, I can say my son is returning to the sheepfold with guidance by our pastor (a spiritual head). He is living in his own house, working a full-time job, paying tithes and returning to college at the age of 20 years old. My son even puts money in my bank account every payday while supplying me with a cell phone. He has not preached his first sermon yet but when he does I will be right there supporting him and giving God all the glory! I am thankful that God guards the feet of His saints, but the wicked shall be silent in darkness. For by strength no man shall prevail. The adversaries of the Lord shall be broken in pieces; from Heaven He will thunder against them (1 Samuel 2:9-10).

Chapter Seven

Another level...
"The thief cometh not but for to steal, and to kill and to destroy: I am come that they might have life, and that they might have it more abundantly" (John 10:10).
Her entire world crashed one cold December morning in 1998. She was tucked into bed last night; she never knew that her mother would not be around to greet her in the morning. There were no warning or signs of goodbyes between them. Just a rude awakening in her life...she had no choice but to go on with life...with a written letter left to her by her mother...saying I love you because I knew my death was coming, baby.
*I pray, Lord, rescue Her from distress, please! You knew her before the foundations of the earth, "**Your Daughter of Destiny.**"*

In 1994, returning to my old neighborhood, driving through the streets that I'd walked long ago, seeing former classmates and reliving my roots gave me fond memories of my oldest sister who was also home. She had given birth to another child since we'd last seen each other and this was the first time I'd seen my new niece. Not to mention, my older sister had not seen my children due to a ten-year time frame of not having seen each other. She had gotten married and I was a teenager, approaching high school graduation and college bound when she moved away. It was nice to go back home and visit. I was the child that left my hometown to move an hour and 45 minutes away.

I went to my parents' home to see all of the changes which they'd done in the home. Since my sister moved back in town I ventured over to her house; we were happy to see other. It was nice to muse over our lives and see each other's children. Life had been good to us as we reminisced into hours of the night. It was late night when the children were sleeping that my sister revealed to me she was dying and wanted me to get to know my niece. She wanted me to raise her once she was deceased. I thought my sister had been drinking too much or was just joking.

When we had gotten settled into our apartment and I had a job, my sister cared for my children. We began to rebuild our bond of closeness. My children became acquainted with their auntie and developed a close relationship with their youngest cousin. She was just turning two years old and loved throwing chicken bones at her older cousins. She was famous for smashing cookies in her cousins' hair and scratching their faces. Nevertheless, they developed bonds on their own levels between each other and family unity grew among them. Soon our children were accustomed to seeing each other every day. We lived in the same neighborhood, just around the corner from each other, and supported our children in their extracurricular activities. My daughter had her first dance recital and my sister and I attended. We prepared to attend with new outfits and fresh flowers for the recital, but little did we all know what was awaiting us at five o'clock, the very next morning.

We were awakened to a loud banging on our apartment door the next morning. It was my sister's boyfriend, letting us know that the paramedics were attempting to revive my sister. Panic hit all three of us at once. My daughter and son left the house before me. I arrived around the corner to see the cardiac unit on the scene. Having been in the medical field, I was aware of what was coming next. In the apartment, my sister was not responding and they called the code. There were so many questions running through my mind like what was I to tell her daughter? How was I supposed to explain to her that her mother was gone? Who was going to fill this empty void in her child's life? I was glad that my children were there to help me through this period of getting my niece dressed and fed. I put her furniture back in place in the living room. Naturally, I had to make calls to the family. Strangely my niece was acting as though nothing had happened to her mother. She didn't even ask about her. She actually thought that her mother had prepared breakfast earlier. The funeral day was fast approaching as everyone focused on themselves. My niece temporarily lived with her grandmother and was later sent to live with a close family friend who specialized in mental health.

It was 2001, after moving to Arizona that I received a call from Virginia stating my niece was in custody. My niece arrived to live with us in June of 2001. That's when another level began in my life. Apparently my niece had behavioral issues in school, a mouth like a sailor, and major anger problems, diagnosed as attention deficit disorder. What had I gotten myself into? This nine-year-old child was a handful from sunrise to sunset. I was thankful for her medication which knocked her out in the evening. There were times when we would find her sitting over in the corner nodding out with her head back. Every day there were phone calls from the school regarding her disorderly conduct and disrespect for authority. Finally, she was placed in special education class and what a coincidence to find that the same year her principal retired early. At first, I thought this was just a stage that my niece was going through, maybe an adjustment to relocating. I worked so much that I was not home and did not see her behavior firsthand. Then I made excuses for her misbehavior like she just needed time to deal with her mother's death and her father's absence. Finally, I began to face the reality of my niece's demeanor. These behavior patterns were not normal, they were not going to change, and she enjoyed the negative attention.

I was confused. She had been manipulating all of us or was she in need of deliverance (freedom from addictive behaviors)? Jesus let us know the reason he came to earth. Luke 4:18 says, "The Spirit of the Lord is upon me, because he hath anointed me to preach the gospel to the poor; he hath sent me to heal the brokenhearted, to preach deliverance to the captives and recovering of sight to the blind, to set at liberty them that are bruised." These behaviors should have left her when she was younger. Now that she was getting older, these bad habits had become addictive behaviors. These behaviors had formed a pattern of being disruptive and out of control. I noticed that my niece had some characteristics that the Bible spoke against. I had realized that the Lord is the Spirit, and where the Spirit of the Lord is there is liberty (II Corinthians 3:17). My niece did not follow rules or regulations. She was very rebellious and disobedient to everybody. For rebellion is as the sin of witchcraft, and stubbornness is as iniquity and idolatry. Because thou hast rejected the word of the Lord, he has also rejected thee from being king (I Samuel 15:23).

I realized that my niece needed mass deliverance from her past. She had ancestral and generational issues which needed prayer and covering in the word, as well as consecration. One of the mothers of the church said, "Through wisdom a house is built, and by understanding it is established" (Proverbs 24:3). I had to go back over my niece's life and find every behavior which was from her father and mother. Then I wrote them down on paper while writing the opposing spirit opposite from her addictive behavior. For example: for anger the contradictory spirit was peace. After listing the spirits that I observed in my niece, I did the same for my own children. I began to bind the negative spirits and loose the exact opposites. My reason for acting on these spirits in this manner is because the Bible says in Matthew 16:19, "And I will give unto thee the keys of the kingdom of heaven: and whatsoever thou shalt bind on earth shall be bound in heaven: and whatsoever thou shalt loose on earth shall be loosed in heaven."

Next I prayed and asked God to guide me in getting my niece in a position to receive the deliverance that would come at the right time. Also at this time, I was reading books on deliverance, prayers for breakthroughs, children deliverance manuals, healing emotional hurts from life, and anything which would help my niece's emotional liberation. I found myself back in school taking child development courses and learning how to handle the developmentally challenged children. There was a need to better understand what she was experiencing so that I could know what I was up against in order to fight earthly, mentally, spiritually, emotionally and physically. A true soldier is prepared for war. I was not going to allow her life to go down the river without a hard battle. You see I knew what it was like to have the odds of the world against you in life. Society would label you as different and insufficient according to their standards if you gave them the opportunity. I knew that she needed a fervent advocate in her corner. I owed her and her mother that much after all we were family.

It looked as though the more I tried to help my niece, the more trouble she got into at school, at early morning daycare, on the school bus, and in the neighborhood. We would get a call from her school every day for different disorderly actions. If my memory serves me correctly, in one year she was suspended so often that school districts did not want to put up with her behavior in their institutions of higher learning. I began to ask God to help me with this child because she was causing me to lose high-paying positions with major companies. I had run out of babysitters that would take care of her while I worked and while my children went to school. I am going to share a few of her adventures with you or as my children and I used to call them pansies 12's.

Perhaps, the most upsetting bus exploit was when my niece bit the 50-year-old bus driver and stole her leftover lunch. I was shocked by many of her actions, but this one was inexcusable to me. The bus driver could have pressed charges against my niece for assault. She was raised to respect her elders. Furthermore, she was not hungry or denied food so why did she need to steal food. My son had to ride the school bus home for the driver to feel safe from such treatment occurring again; I was outraged. This child had a total of 50 to 60 bus referrals in one year. She was motivation for the transportation department to place cameras on the buses when in operation. When we moved (to a different city limit) the new district did not want to provide her with transportation for three weeks; therefore, I had to take her and pick her up from school. I made sure that I had my niece in church every time the church doors were opened and I made sure she was getting prayer.

Believe it or not as much as I thought my niece loved me, there was a time I doubted the validity of her capability to love. We had just viewed *The Passion of the Christ* after church service and shared Sunday dinner. My son was outside sharing the good word of Jesus Christ, I was taking a nap and my niece was playing in her room. I thank God that my son came into the house. Upon entering he caught her striking matches and throwing them at my bed while I was sleeping. Right then and there I knew this child needed professional help for her mental health. I spoke with elders of the church and prayers went up, fasting also took place with laying on of hands by my pastor and the ministerial staff. I also called on my church family in New York who was in deliverance ministry. They sent me deliverance materials for this battle was not mine but the Lord's. I began to read warfare scriptures for protection. For example: Isaiah 54:17, Colossians 1:13, 2 Timothy 4:18, Psalm 23, Psalm 91, Psalm 109, Psalm 119, 2 Chronicles 16:9, Psalm 35 and many other scriptures. I began to anoint her clothes with blessed oil that was anointed and prayed over by my pastors. Next, I began to consecrate her night clothes and purchase all-white pajamas with white footy socks. At this time, I began to play the Bible tapes reading the book of Acts and Revelation in her bedroom continuously at night. I was instructed that Revelation was a good book because it tells of the victory for the saints over the kingdom of darkness. The book of Acts tells of the Comforter, the Holy Spirit baptizing with fire for the saints of God. By this time, my son and I were in seminary school two nights a week and at times she attended the classes with us. My niece was wrapped in the word of God constantly for two years.

There were definite outbursts when the word of God was fed to her constantly, yet she still misbehaved. The police would bring her home for stealing from the store. I then decided that if I caught her with stolen merchandise I'd immediately return her along with the merchandise to the store! I would call the police and request for them to place her in the back of the car in handcuffs. She was then placed in a program where she spent a weekend in a scared straight program. She thought that I was joking, but I dropped her right off at the juvenile detention center. When I pulled up on the property my niece tried to play hard, but I left her there for an overnight experience and did not look back. My niece was the youngest child to attend this program; but I knew that there was always hope if she was shown tough love. There comes a time when we as parents and guardians have to make difficult decisions in order to help children face reality. Nevertheless, I took my niece on a national television show for troubled children. She was seen stealing money from a locker on a live show. This opened doors for her to attend a school that handled children with behavioral issues. For a while that school assisted her by providing increased school attendance, disciplined educational settings, behavioral coaches with therapeutic hands-on maneuvers, and re-directional techniques for behavioral children.

Currently, my niece continues learning how to cope with her behavior but realities of life are providing her with lessons she will never forget. She has a prayer life, reads scripture daily, gets in the prayer line for anointed laying on of hands for her own deliverance, anoints herself with blessed oil daily, takes medication for her moods, admits to personality conflicts and wants to get help so she can eventually be a functional person in society. Many activities of daily living like washing clothes, household chores and cooking are preparing her for her own self-sufficiency. I believe that when she makes up her mind and wants to enjoy her life as a productive citizen that she will be able to function at any level of life. I know that when she is ready for total deliverance that also is available for her. For we know that God is a gentleman. We have the right of free will to come in and partake with Him by open invitation extended through Jesus Christ.

I have a supportive family, fervent praying women anchored in God, a resourceful team of mental health specialists, and powerful warrior men of God on my team. Along with such God-connected sisters and brothers, constantly seeking for more knowledge in deliverance has provided me with solid biblical methods explained for our children's success. I recently discovered that we as parental heads can do more than pray and speak deliverance over our children, we can decree it. For example: like in the book of Esther victory is ours. We can write the vision and make it plain. We can reverse ancestral and generational bondage by more than just binding and loosing, we can decree deliverance for our children, too. We must continue to take back what the enemy stole from us by all means necessary, which is stated in our Bibles. Today, I have decreed all of my children's deliverance. I have proclaimed that me and my house shall serve the Lord. I have laid down the law (decreed) that my children are set free from ancestral and generational bondage. For all of my family members are new creatures in Jesus Christ and have life more abundantly. My children are the head and not the tail because the fruit of all saved women are blessed. All I am suggesting to mothers out there is to get before God and fight the good fight of faith for your children and know that we may hurt for a minute but joy will come in the morning time. Even when it looks as though the enemy is winning, realize that at the name of Jesus Christ every opposing situation has already been won. It was done over 2,000 years ago on Calvary.

Just to encourage mothers who seem to be in extremely difficult situations. Be of good cheer and know that God will bring you out just like in Exodus 14. I was in this major storm and from time to time I would see God parting the waters while I walked on dry land with the waters up high on my left and right sides. I would even see my enemy pursuing me from the rear but God made a way for me and gave me the victory in His time. Amen.

My niece turned a small town upside down with her rebellious and disrespectful behavior from the months of August to May. Authorities in the town did not believe me when I advised that she needed to be placed in a full residential behavioral center for restructuring of her learned behaviors. All of the family agencies, school officials, even some church members thought that I was exaggerating and just could not handle my niece. When she left out of my door from up under this anointing that God placed in my home, she grew worse. It took a matter of three weeks for all who doubted me to see that I knew what I was talking about with this child. After caring for her in my home for six years, I knew every operating behavior she had and when each behavior would become active.

Please, believe me when I tell you I was tormented verbally by people who did not believe me. I was ostracized by neighbors, disliked by many professionals and frowned upon by health care personnel but God brought me through all of the trials of opposition. I was so broken with such a contrite heart that I think my family members, support team, church family and my family advocate believed along with me that I was going to lose my mind. I was filled with spirits of doubt, confusion, double-mindedness, insecurity, low self-esteem, stress and crying constantly. When the enemy attempted to come in like a flood to drown me, God raised up a standard against the enemy and brought forth victory. My niece is currently in a full residential behavioral youth center receiving the therapeutic treatment to assist her in having abundant life. It was a rough road, but know that if God did it for the Israelites, Job, the three Hebrew boys, Daniel, Peter, Paul, Silas, John and everyone else God will do the same for you. God is no respector of person. Standing is easily said out of our mouths and hard to actually do but nothing good nor beneficial comes easy; there is work involved in all things. We must do the natural and God will do the supernatural. Mothers, take the advice from another mother, take God's hand and walk through those valleys in life. Thanking God every step of the way. We must praise God and watch the enemy get removed out of our very path.

Chapter Eight

Mothers, hurt no more
It is has been decreed in Proverbs 31:28a:
Her children arise up, and call her blessed; (KJV)
It has been decreed that women are excellent mothers due their reverence for God.
REMEMBER TO DECREE: As for Me and My House We Shall Serve the Lord! AMEN

Mothers have positions ranging from store clerks to CEOs of companies. Mothers are to be measured by their attractiveness in character, not just physical beauty. Daughters, rise up and be inspired by mothers and use them as examples for your role as a mother. Let your mothers know you appreciate them in spite of all the rough times and difficult situations. Admire how mothers overcame trials and tribulations while we grew up as children. Simply stated love, respect, honor and appreciate your mother while you have her around to share positive affection.

Finally, I am sharing this with you mothers so that you will not go through these hurts aimlessly and without any sense of assurance and faith as I did. I'm praying that you will know how to fight the enemy with your sword (the word of God) and hold on to God in victory after sharing my experiences with you! For my Bible tells me that we are to be helpers one to another. If we can help each other by sharing what we've gone through then that is our job.

Somewhere out there mothers are hurting and they are blindly reaching out for help in desperation. It's amazing that no one has taken the time to say do this or do that in a step-by-step process. We are our brothers' and sisters' keepers! Look at Genesis 4:9-10 where God makes it plain that we are responsible for each other, or do you want your brother's blood crying out to God? Beware that when we fall short of doing this, we are acting like a *defector of Heaven*, because even Judas Iscariot (seen as a betrayer of Jesus Christ at the last supper) did not scam on his God-given assignment. His God-given purpose was to betray Jesus Christ for 30 pieces of silver, according to prophesy. This was his job although at times we did not like his occupation. The question is did he fulfill his appointment? We are no different than Judas; we must complete our God-given assignment, too. My advice is to do what God has instructed you do in life, for obedience is better than sacrifice. My goal is for the Lord to say, "Well done, thy good and faithful servant."

My prayer is for these words in this book to touch those that need to be touched; reaching those that need reaching, right in the midst of their dilemmas. Allowing them to be fed by God, making it out of those predicaments with their children and loved ones. Saints of the Most High God, should always call on God and fight with the sword, which is the word of God, as stated in Ephesians chapter 6. Mothers should use the sword to cut sharper into their life situations; the sword (Word of God) reveals how to use power when speaking to the mountains in life. This is also the key essential for moving towards resolution and deliverance. Spreading this experience is the one sure way of reassuring family restoration and a prosperous growth of unity in the Lord God, our Savior. Please, remember it is in our weakness that God is most powerful! No hurt, harm, nor danger shall befall you for God is in the midst!

Be blessed and know that whatever you are going through God knows and He is there with you...just talk to Him (build that relationship with your Heavenly Father, He is waiting) ... I know, I have tried it and He has been nothing but good to me.

Be he that knew not, and did commit things worthy of stripes, shall be beaten with few stripes for unto whosoever much is given, of him shall much be required: and to whom men have committed much, of him they will ask the more (Luke 12:48).

Appendix A

Encyclopedia of Life Application Articles

On the following pages you will find God's Word on mothers' qualities, mothers' responsibilities, how to treat your mother and God's promises regarding our parents. All of this information came from iLumina Gold Software By Benny Hinn Ministries. Tyndale House Publishers, 2003. This word of God's addresses vital issues regarding mothers. Please, refer to this information in time of need and/or direction.

Mothers, God's Word on What Are the Qualities a Mother Should Possess?

1 Kings 3:26-27—Then the woman who really was the mother of the living child, and who loved him very much, cried out, "Oh no, my lord! Give her the child—please do not kill him!" But the other woman said, "All right, he will be neither yours nor mine; divide him between us!" Then the king said, "Do not kill him, but give the baby to the woman who wants him to live, for she is his mother!" A wise mother should love her children unselfishly, wanting what is best for the child above what is best for her.

1 Thessalonians 2:7—As apostles of Christ we certainly had a right to make some demands of you, but we were as gentle among you as a mother feeding and caring for her own children. A wise mother is gentle with her children

Hebrews 11:23—It was by faith that Moses' parents hid him for three months. They saw that God had given them an unusual child, and they were not afraid of what the king might do. A wise mother exercises great faith for her children.

Proverbs 14:1—A wise woman builds her house; a foolish woman tears hers down with her own hands. A wise mother builds her family up rather than tearing them down with hurtful words.

What Are Some of the Responsibilities of a Mother?

Proverbs 4:3—I, too, was once my father's son, tenderly loved by my mother as an only child. A mother should love her children.

Luke 18:15—One day some parents brought their little children to Jesus so he could touch them and bless them, but the disciples told them not to bother him. A mother should lead her children to Jesus.

2 Timothy 1:50—I know that you sincerely trust the Lord, for you have the faith of your mother, Eunice, and your grandmother, Lois. A mother should be a woman with great faith in God which can become a great heritage for her family.

Deuteronomy 8:5—You should realize that just as a parent disciplines a child, the Lord your God disciplines you to help you. A wise mother disciplines her children with the same loving hand the Lord shows to her.

Proverbs 1:8—Listen, my child, to what your father teaches you. Don't neglect your mother's teaching. A mother teaches her children God's way.

Isaiah 66:12-13—"Peace and prosperity will overflow Jerusalem like a river," says the Lord. "The wealth of the nations will flow to her. Her children will be nursed at her breasts, carried in her arms, and treated with love. I will comfort you there as a child is comforted by its mother." A mother comforts her children.

Mark 10:7—This explains why a man leaves his father and mother and is joined to his wife. A mother raises her children to become mature and independent young people.

How Am I to Treat My Mother?

Exodus 20:12—"Honor your father and mother. Then you will live a long, full life in the land the Lord your God will give you."

Leviticus 19:3—Each of you must show respect for your mother and father, and you must always observe my Sabbath days of rest, for I, the Lord, am your God. Honor and respect your mother, as God commands.

John 19:26-27—When Jesus saw his mother standing there beside the disciple he loved, he said to her, "Woman, he is your son." And he said to this disciple, "She is your mother." And from then on this disciple took her into his home.

Matthew 15:5—You say, "You don't need to honor your parents by caring for their needs if you give the money to God instead."

1 Timothy 5:3-4—The church should care for any widow who has no one else to care for her. But if she has children or grandchildren, their first responsibility is to show godliness at home and repay their parents by taking care of them. Provide for your mother and care for her.

Proverbs 31:28—Her children stand and bless her. Her husband praises her. Bless and praise your mother.

Proverbs 19:26—Children who mistreat their father or chase away their mother are a public disgrace and an embarrassment.

Proverbs 20:20—If you curse your father or mother, the lamp of your life will be snuffed out.

Proverbs 30:11—Some people curse their father and do not thank their mother. Treat your mother with kindness and thankfulness.

Proverbs 23:22-25—Don't despise your mother's experience when she is old. Get the truth and don't ever sell it; also get wisdom, discipline, and discernment. The father of godly children has cause for joy. What a pleasure it is to have wise children. So give your parents joy! May she who gave you birth be happy. Bring joy to your mother by being a wise child

Promise from God
Exodus 20:12—"Honor your father and mother. Then you will live a long, full life in the land the Lord your God will give you."

***Mothers**, grasp that God does not mean for you to be abused by your children in any way, form or fashion. Should you be experiencing abuse from a child whether it is violent, disrespectful shouting, pushing, destroying your walls, property out of anger speak out against it, get protection for yourself by law enforcement, contact social service offices, seek the department of juvenile justice or any resource available for your safety. DO NOT accept abuse God did not intend for you, too. Jesus Christ came so that we may have life and more abundantly. Amen.*

CPSIA information can be obtained
at www.ICGtesting.com
Printed in the USA
LVOW11s1230290117
522514LV00004B/321/P